Supernatural Identity

Power-Packed Quotes
To Help You Revolutionize Your Life!

Harrison House
Tulsa, Oklahoma

Unless otherwise indicated, all Scripture quotations are taken from the *King James Version* of the Bible.

Initial Scripture compilation was provided by Terry Lawson.

Supernatural Identity — Power-Packed Quotes
To Help You Revolutionize Your Life!
ISBN 0-89274-949-0
Copyright © 1996 by Harrison House, Inc.
P. O. Box 35035
Tulsa, Oklahoma 74153

Contents

Introduction

This book is a unique collection of quotes that will help establish you in your identity in Christ. These quotes come from Spirit-filled men and women such as Kenneth E. Hagin, Joyce Meyer, Kenneth Copeland, Gloria Copeland, Marilyn Hickey, Frederick K. C. Price, Billy Joe Daugherty, Smith Wigglesworth, John G. Lake and Kathryn Kuhlman who have learned what it means to be in Him. Each quote is coupled with a Scripture so that you will be able to see for yourself what God says about you and has for you in His Word.

With these quotes and Scriptures, you can begin to renew your mind to what God's Word says about: provision, health, eternal life, oneness with God, a new nature, forgiveness, righteousness, the Holy Spirit and His fruit, the wisdom of God, fellowship with the Father, dominion over circumstances, authority, power and victory. Take this opportunity to find out who you are in Christ. If you do, it will revolutionize your life!

*P*raise be to the God and Father of our Lord Jesus Christ, who has blessed us in the heavenly realms with every spiritual blessing in Christ.

EPHESIANS 1:3 NIV

As far as God is concerned everything you have or are "in Christ" is so. He has done it. Everything the Bible says is ours, is ours legally.

KENNETH E. HAGIN

We having the same spirit of faith, according as it is written, I believed, and therefore have I spoken; we also believe, and therefore speak.

2 Corinthians 4:13

God wants us to believe with our heart and say with our lips all He says we are in Christ. We are not to ignore or neglect our legal standing in Christ.

F. F. Bosworth

1
Provision in Christ

But my God shall supply all your need according to his riches in glory by Christ Jesus.

PHILIPPIANS 4:19

In Christ, all of my needs are provided for.

In whom we have redemption through his blood, the forgiveness of sins, according to the riches of his grace.

EPHESIANS 1:7

If you have a working revelation of your redemption in Christ Jesus, there is not one prayer that needs to go unanswered or any need that has to go unmet.

KENNETH COPELAND

God is able to bless you with ample means, so that you may always have quite enough for any emergency of your own and ample besides for any kind act to others.

2 CORINTHIANS 9:8 MOFFATT

There is no insufficiency in Jesus. His grace is sufficient in all circumstances.

JOHN OSTEEN

*F*or it is in him, and in him alone, that all the treasures of wisdom and knowledge lie hidden.

COLOSSIANS 2:3 PHILLIPS

All of the knowledge to solve every one of those needs is in God and He is in you.

T. L. OSBORN

The thief cometh not, but for to steal, and to kill, and to destroy: I am come that they might have life, and that they might have it more abundantly.

JOHN 10:10

Jesus paid the price for you to live the abundant life . . . . He has made plenty of provision for victory and peace and abundance in every area of your life.

NORVEL HAYES

*T*his means that he can save fully and completely those who approach God through him, for he is always living to intercede on their behalf.

HEBREWS 7:25 PHILLIPS

All that we receive from the Father must come through Jesus Christ the Son, and that is why at the heart of our faith is a person — the very Son of the very God.

KATHRYN KUHLMAN

Giving thanks to the Father, Who made us meet for the portion of the inheritance of the saints in light.

COLOSSIANS 1:12 WORRELL

My heritage is to have God's best, to enjoy His companionship and to use His wealth and power for the good of myself and others.

T. L. OSBORN

And of his fulness have all we received, and grace for grace.

JOHN 1:16

Grace is always dependent on who and what God is, never on who and what man is. God blesses us on His merits, not ours.

BOB YANDIAN

And since children, also heirs; on the one hand, heirs of God, on the other, joint-heirs with Christ.

ROMANS 8:17 WUEST

We have equal inheritance with our brother Jesus Christ . . . everything He has is ours to share.

BUDDY HARRISON

*F*or all of you who had yourselves baptized into Christ have taken on the character of Christ.

GALATIANS 3:27 MOFFATT

Because you are in Christ Jesus, you can live like Him.

KENNETH COPELAND

When Christ, who is our life, shall appear, then shall ye also appear with him in glory.

COLOSSIANS 3:4

Our lives are supposed to be centered on Jesus. If you will order your life by His life, you will experience abundant living.

FREDERICK K. C. PRICE

But he who joins himself to the Lord is one spirit [with Him].

1 CORINTHIANS 6:17 WUEST

You are called a joint-heir with Christ Jesus. You are in Him. God sees you in Jesus. He not only comes inside you, but you went inside Him.

KENNETH COPELAND

2
Healing in Christ

Who his own self bare our sins in his own body on the tree, that we, being dead to sins, should live unto righteousness: by whose stripes ye were healed.

1 PETER 2:24

In Christ, healing belongs to me.

*A*nd thus He fulfilled what was spoken by the prophet Isaiah, He Himself took [in order to carry away] our weaknesses and infirmities and bore away our diseases.

MATTHEW 8:17 AMP

By His stripes I was healed! If I was healed then I am healed. Healing belongs to me because I am in Christ.

KENNETH E. HAGIN

Calling the twelve apostles together, he gave them power and authority over all demons as well as to heal diseases.

LUKE 9:1 MOFFATT

If you stand on God's Word in the name of Jesus, the devil has to obey you. . . . Jesus gave us all power and authority over demons and diseases.

NORVEL HAYES

*F*or those God foreknew he also predestined to be conformed to the likeness of his Son, that he might be the firstborn among many brothers.

ROMANS 8:29 NIV

You are a three-part being — spirit, soul, and body; and God intends for you to be like Him in every area of your being.

MARILYN HICKEY

. . . but with God all things are possible.

MATTHEW 19:26

There are no hopeless cases with God. There are no incurable diseases with God. There are no unsolvable problems with God.

ORAL ROBERTS

*F*or we are members of his body,
of his flesh, and of his bones.

EPHESIANS 5:30

In becoming part of the Body of Christ, sickness
should have no more mastery over us than it had
over the Body of Christ when He was on earth.

GORDON LINDSAY

Therefore we are buried with him by baptism into death: that like as Christ was raised up from the dead by the glory of the Father, even so we also should walk in newness of life.

ROMANS 6:4

When Jesus Christ arose in a new life, you arose to walk in that same new life of God.

T. L. OSBORN

Because through Christ Jesus the law of the Spirit of life set me free from the law of sin and death.

ROMANS 8:2 NIV

That law of the Spirit of life in Christ will set you free from sin and death because you have Christ in you.

MARILYN HICKEY

Who his own self bare our sins in his own body on the tree, that we, being dead to sins, should live unto righteousness: by whose stripes ye were healed.

1 PETER 2:24

Being in Christ means that you are "the healed." He was made sick with our sickness; but He didn't stay sick. He is healed; and because we are in Him, we are healed, too!

KENNETH COPELAND

3
Life Eternal in Christ

And this is the record, that God hath given to us eternal life, and this life is in his Son.

He that hath the Son hath life; and he that hath not the Son of God hath not life.

1 JOHN 5:11, 12

In Christ, I have eternal life.

*T*o them God has chosen to make known among the Gentiles the glorious riches of this mystery, which is Christ in you, the hope of glory.

COLOSSIANS 1:27 NIV

Since Jesus lives inside us, we believers are bigger within than without. Even when this outer shell has crumbled into dust, the inner man will keep on living with the Lord Jesus forever and ever.

BOB YANDIAN

*F*or the law of the Spirit of life in Christ Jesus hath made me free from the law of sin and death.

ROMANS 8:2

Jesus Christ arrested the process of death by the power of God, through the introduction of the life and the Spirit of life in Jesus Christ, giving man eternal life.

JOHN G. LAKE

And now he has made all of this plain to us by the coming of our Savior Jesus Christ, who broke the power of death and showed us the way of everlasting life through trusting him.

2 TIMOTHY 1:10 TLB

Life and immortality are ours in the Gospel. This is our inheritance through the blood of Jesus, life forevermore.

SMITH WIGGLESWORTH

By so much also hath Jesus become the surety of a better covenant.

HEBREWS 7:22 WORRELL

We have a covenant agreement with Almighty God, signed and sealed in the blood of Jesus Who is its guarantee and surety.

JERRY SAVELLE

I am the gate; whoever enters through me will be saved. He will come in and go out, and find pasture.

JOHN 10:9 NIV

There is only one way to heaven. . . . It's through Jesus . . . the door! Jesus is the way.

CHARLES CAPPS

4
A New Creation in Christ

Therefore if any man be in Christ, he is a new creature: old things are passed away; behold, all things are become new.

2 CORINTHIANS 5:17

In Christ, I am a new creation.

But in Christ it is not circumcision or uncircumcision that counts but the power of new birth.

GALATIANS 6:15 PHILLIPS

A Christian is not renovated like a mattress. He is a new creature. He is not just made over. He is a new creation — something which never before existed.

KENNETH E. HAGIN

*F*or we are his workmanship, created in Christ Jesus unto good works, which God hath before ordained that we should walk in them.

EPHESIANS 2:10

God can take a man and give to that man a spiritual healing where he will experience an instantaneous deliverance, and actually be a "new person in Christ Jesus"!

KATHRYN KUHLMAN

Therefore if any man be in Christ, he is a new creature: old things are passed away; behold, all things are become new.

2 CORINTHIANS 5:17

Instead of loving holiness, unregenerate man has a vicious bent toward sin and evil, and only the grace of God can overcome this evil nature, by making Him a "new creature" in Christ.

P. C. NELSON

You have been born anew, not of mortal parentage but of immortal, through the living and enduring word of God.

1 PETER 1:23 NEB

We are no longer mere men, but supernatural men, exactly like Jesus. We got that way by being born again of a supernatural God.

BUDDY HARRISON

*F*or neither is circumcision any-thing, nor uncircumcision, but a new creation.

GALATIANS 6:15 WORRELL

You are a new creature. God is your source, but He has given you the ability and all the necessary ingredients to succeed.

FREDERICK K. C. PRICE

41

*F*or he has rescued us from the dominion of darkness and brought us into the kingdom of the Son he loves.

COLOSSIANS 1:13 NIV

By the new birth you have passed out of Satan's dominion and Satan's power and you have come over into God's dominion.

JOHN G. LAKE

There is a new creation whenever a man comes to be in Christ; what is old is gone, the new has come.

2 CORINTHIANS 5:17 MOFFATT

Being born again by the Spirit of God puts us in a different dimension, a new level, a league by ourselves. We truly have a new identity.

BUDDY HARRISON

Let us never forget that our old selves died with him on the cross that the tyranny of sin over us might be broken.

ROMANS 6:6 PHILLIPS

As far as God is concerned, the sinful nature has been rendered inoperative, but it is up to us to see the new nature manifested outwardly.

FREDERICK K. C. PRICE

*F*or the law of the Spirit of life in Christ Jesus hath made me free from the law of sin and death.

ROMANS 8:2

Through Christ you have been born again and given a new nature so that you can live freely in life rather than living under the bondage of sin and death.

MARILYN HICKEY

The antiquated, out-of-date things [which do not belong to the new life in Christ Jesus] have passed away. Behold, all things have become new in quality.

2 CORINTHIANS 5:17 WUEST

Healing, strength, success, and victory are all a part of this new creation life that has been made a reality by God's imparting His nature to us.

E. W. KENYON

When someone becomes a Christian he becomes a brand new person inside. He is not the same any more. A new life has begun!

2 CORINTHIANS 5:17 TLB

God, through Christ, gives you a chance to make a new start.

FREDERICK K. C. PRICE

5
One With the Father
in Christ

I *and my Father are one.*

JOHN 10:30

*A**t that day ye shall know that I am in my Father, and ye in me, and I in you.*

JOHN 14:20

In Christ, I have been made one with the Father.

But he that is joined unto the Lord is one spirit.

1 CORINTHIANS 6:17

The new birth has brought us into vital union with Jesus Christ.

JOHN G. LAKE

*T*o whom God would make known what is the riches of the glory of this mystery among the Gentiles; which is Christ in you, the hope of glory.

COLOSSIANS 1:27

The life of God is within you. Jesus Himself is living inside you. Everywhere you go, He goes.

GLORIA COPELAND

Baptized into union with him, you have all put on Christ as a garment.

GALATIANS 3:27 NEB

At the point of faith in Christ, God places us in union with Christ. We are accepted in the beloved.

BOB YANDIAN

While he who joins himself to the Lord is one with him in spirit.

1 CORINTHIANS 6:17 MOFFATT

If we were as conscious of our identification with Jesus Christ and our oneness with Him as we are conscious of physical pain and physical need, we would never have pain and we would never mention our needs again.

E. W. KENYON

Ye are of God, little children, and have overcome them: because greater is he that is in you, than he that is in the world.

1 JOHN 4:4

We have been born again with the nature of God. We are one spirit with the Lord. The Greater One lives in us.

GLORIA COPELAND

6
Forgiven in Christ

. . . Christ died for our sins according to the scriptures.

1 Corinthians 15:3

In Christ, I am forgiven of my sins.

There is therefore now no condemnation to them which are in Christ Jesus, who walk not after the flesh, but after the Spirit.

ROMANS 8:1

You are "in Christ" now. There is "no condemnation" in you or toward you from God. You are free from fear. You are liberated from guilt — no matter what you have done or where you have been.

BILLY JOE DAUGHERTY

*F*or the law of the Spirit of life in Christ Jesus hath made me free from the law of sin and death.

ROMANS 8:2

The law of the Spirit of life in Christ Jesus has made us free from the law of sin and death. Those who have Christ do not have to be affected by the law of sin and death.

NORVEL HAYES

*T*herefore, since we are now justified (acquitted, made righteous, and brought into right relationship with God) by Christ's blood, how much more [certain is it that] we shall be saved by Him from the indignation and wrath of God.

ROMANS 5:9 AMP

You must realize that God doesn't see you the way you see yourself. If you are born again, God sees you through the blood of His Son, Jesus. He is not looking at you alone; He sees you in Christ.

CREFLO DOLLAR

It is in him that you reach your full life, and he is the Head of every angelic Ruler and Power.

COLOSSIANS 2:10 MOFFATT

To the man who looks into this perfect law of God all darkness is removed and he sees his completeness in Christ.

SMITH WIGGLESWORTH

If we confess our sins, he is faithful and just to forgive us our sins, and to cleanse us from all unrighteousness.

1 John 1:9

Because of what Christ has done for us, we can go before God, confess our sin, and receive forgiveness of that sin.

JERRY SAVELLE

*T*herefore being justified by faith, we have peace with God through our Lord Jesus Christ.

ROMANS 5:1

By simple faith, belief in God's Son, and acceptance of Him as divine Saviour, the guilty sinner is made righteous.

KATHRYN KUHLMAN

*T*herefore, there is now no condemnation for those who are in Christ Jesus.

ROMANS 8:1 NIV

There is a place for us in Christ Jesus where we are no longer under condemnation but where the heavens are always open to us.

SMITH WIGGLESWORTH

Much more then, having now been justified by His blood, we shall be saved from the wrath of God through Him.

ROMANS 5:9 NAS

When Jesus washes your sins away you are declared righteous by God Himself. If you're saved, you're one of the "just."

CREFLO DOLLAR

To open their eyes, and to turn them from darkness to light, and from the power of Satan unto God, that they may receive forgiveness of sins, and inheritance among them which are sanctified by faith that is in me.

ACTS 26:18

God purposed that every newborn babe in Christ was called to be a saint; called from the darkness to light, from the power of Satan unto God.

SMITH WIGGLESWORTH

7
Righteous in Christ

For he hath made him to be sin for us, who knew no sin; that we might be made the righteousness of God in him.

2 CORINTHIANS 5:21

In Christ, I am in right standing with God and declared righteous.

*E*ven the righteousness of God which is by faith of Jesus Christ unto all and upon all them that believe: for there is no difference.

ROMANS 3:22

As a born-again child of God you not only have the righteousness of God, you are the righteousness of God.

CREFLO DOLLAR

. . . He chose us in him ere the world was founded, to be consecrated and unblemished in his sight, destining us in love to be his sons through Jesus Christ.

EPHESIANS 1:4, 5 MOFFATT

You are in the Body of Christ here on earth. In the eyes of God you are holy and blameless, beyond reproach and without rebuke.

KENNETH COPELAND

For God took the sinless Christ and poured into him our sins. Then, in exchange, he poured God's goodness into us!

2 CORINTHIANS 5:21 TLB

If you have been washed in the blood of Jesus Christ, then you are not "an old sinner." You have been given a new identity... you have been made the righteousness of God in Him.

JERRY SAVELLE

*A*nd of his fulness have all we received, and grace for grace.

JOHN 1:16

We died once with Christ. Now we live with Him, we reign with Him. His perfect righteousness is ours. All He is and did is ours.

E. W. KENYON

It is God's way of righting wrong, effective through faith in Christ for all who have such faith — all, without distinction.

ROMANS 3:22 NEB

If Jesus is your Lord, then you are in right-standing with God — you have the righteousness of God. You have a right to everything which God has.

KENNETH COPELAND

69

*F*or our sake He made Christ [virtually] to be sin Who knew no sin, so that in and through Him we might become [endued with, viewed as being in, and examples of] the righteousness of God [what we ought to be, approved and acceptable and in right relationship with Him, by His goodness].

2 CORINTHIANS 5:21 AMP

We are the righteousness of God in Christ Jesus. God's righteousness cannot be inferior or unworthy.

CHARLES CAPPS

To the praise of the glory of His grace, which He freely bestowed on us in the Beloved.

EPHESIANS 1:6 NAS

The reason we praise God the Father is because He has made us accepted in His Son Jesus Christ [the Beloved].

BOB YANDIAN

To put on the clean fresh clothes of the new life which was made by God's design for righteousnes and the holiness which is no illusion.

EPHESIANS 4:24 PHILLIPS

In God's eyes we are clothed in robes of righteousness which are white and spotless.

BUDDY HARRISON

Christ was innocent of sin, and yet for our sake God made him one with the sinfulness of men, so that in him we might be made one with the goodness of God himself.

2 CORINTHIANS 5:21 NEB

Replace negative thoughts and words with positive ones. Stop seeing yourself as an unworthy sinner, see yourself as the righteousness of God in Christ Jesus.

JOYCE MEYER

8
The Holy Spirit's Presence Through Christ

But the fruit of the [Holy] Spirit [the work which His presence within accomplishes] is love, joy (gladness), peace, patience (an even temper, forbearance), kindness, goodness (benevolence), faithfulness, Gentleness (meekness, humility), self-control (self-restraint, continence). Against such things there is no law [that can bring a charge].   GALATIANS 5:22, 23 AMP

In Christ, the presence of the Holy Spirit in my life causes me to bear good fruit.

*H*ereby know we that we dwell in him, and he in us, because he hath given us of his Spirit.

1 JOHN 4:13

The gift of the Spirit is proof positive that we are accepted in the Beloved, and that we are joint-heirs with Him.

P. C. NELSON

*F*or in Him the whole fullness of Deity (the Godhead) continues to dwell in bodily form [giving complete expression of the divine nature].

And you are in Him, made full and having come to fullness of life . . . .

And He is the Head of all rule and authority [of every angelic principality and power].

COLOSSIANS 2:9, 10 AMP

Christ gave Himself. He gave us His attention, His affection, and His assurance.

T. D. JAKES

Blessed be the God and Father of our Lord Jesus Christ, who hath blessed us with all spiritual blessings in heavenly places in Christ.

EPHESIANS 1:3

Everything we receive must come through Jesus. He's the One . . . He is even the Giver of the Holy Spirit.

KATHRYN KUHLMAN

*T*herefore, my beloved brethren, be ye stedfast, unmoveable, always abounding in the work of the Lord, forasmuch as ye know that your labour is not in vain in the Lord.

1 CORINTHIANS 15:58

It is only as you are filled with the Holy Spirit that you become steadfast and unmovable in Him.

SMITH WIGGLESWORTH

And if the Spirit of him who raised Jesus from the dead is living in you, he who raised Christ from the dead will also give life to your mortal bodies through his Spirit, who lives in you.

ROMANS 8:11 NIV

There is a secret in Jesus Christ. Christianity is all supernatural; every bit of it.

JOHN G. LAKE

*E*ach receives his manifestation of the Spirit for the common good.... But all these effects are produced by one and the same Spirit, apportioning them severally to each individual as he pleases.

1 CORINTHIANS 12:7, 11 MOFFATT

With the Holy Spirit living inside us, we can intercede for the salvation, healing and deliverance of other people. And moved with the compassion of God, we can reach out and let the gifts of the Spirit manifest through us to pour out and bless others' lives.

PAT HARRISON

And the peace of God, which passeth all understanding, shall keep your hearts and minds through Christ Jesus.

PHILIPPIANS 4:7

You can have the peace of God. It has been multiplied unto you through the exact, full knowledge of the Father and of His Son, Jesus Christ.

KEITH BUTLER

9
Wisdom in Christ

But of him are ye in Christ Jesus, who of God is made unto us wisdom, and righteousness, and sanctification, and redemption.

1 Corinthians 1:30

In Christ, I have the wisdom of God.

*F*or the law was given by Moses, but grace and truth came by Jesus Christ.

JOHN 1:17

By the grace of God that came through Jesus Christ, we can be led by the Spirit. We can have the Spirit of wisdom, understanding, counsel, might, knowledge, and the fear of the Lord.

JOHN OSTEEN

*I*f any of you is deficient in wisdom, let him ask of the giving God [Who gives] to everyone liberally and ungrudgingly, without reproaching or faultfinding, and it will be given him.

JAMES 1:5 AMP

God is made wisdom in Christ to us. That means that the wisdom and ability of God is imparted to us in Christ. We have access to it.

E. W. KENYON

*Y*ou are in Christ Jesus by God's act, for God has made him our wisdom; he is our righteousness; in him we are consecrated and set free.

1 CORINTHIANS 1:30 NEB

God made Jesus to be your wisdom through the miraculous union that took place when you were saved. Jesus is your wisdom.

BILLY JOE DAUGHERTY

*B*ut we speak God's wisdom in the form of a mystery long hidden but now revealed and understandable, that wisdom which has been kept secret which God foreordained before the ages with a view to our glory . . . .   1 CORINTHIANS 2:7 WUEST

. . . it is in him [Christ], and in him alone, that all the treasures of wisdom and knowledge lie hidden.

COLOSSIANS 2:3 PHILLIPS

Paul said all wisdom and knowledge are hidden in Christ. To be truly educated, you must be born again, filled with the Holy Spirit, and have your mind renewed with the Word to be able to hear the things of the Lord.   FREDERICK K.C. PRICE

To the intent that now unto the principalities and powers in heavenly places might be known by the church the manifold wisdom of God.

EPHESIANS 3:10

God had a plan which was hidden in Him for a day to come when every believer would be able to show on the earth God's manifold wisdom.

BOB YANDIAN

*F*or it is in him, and in him alone, that all the treasures of wisdom and knowledge lie hidden.

COLOSSIANS 2:3 PHILLIPS

All that God created for His children, in the beginning, is now restored to you through Jesus Christ.

T. L. OSBORN

*T*hat the God of our Lord Jesus Christ, the Father of glory, may give unto you the spirit of wisdom and revelation in the knowledge of him.

EPHESIANS 1:17

A man who has God in him will have wisdom. At every crisis of his day's work, he has the One inside Who knows all. He learns the secret of leaning back upon the One inside.

E. W. KENYON

*B*ut of Him are ye in Christ Jesus, Who was made to us wisdom from God, also righteousness, and holiness, and redemption.

1 Corinthians 1:30 Worrell

Wisdom comes from an encounter with the Christ Who is the wisdom of God. Success in life requires a solid edifice of wisdom and knowledge built upon a stable foundation of truth that cannot be swayed.

Dick Mills

10
Fellowship in Christ

. . . Holy Father, keep through thine own name those whom thou hast given me, that they may be one, as we are.

JOHN 17:11

In Christ, I have fellowship with the Father.

I am crucified with Christ: nevertheless I live; yet not I, but Christ liveth in me: and the life which I now live in the flesh I live by the faith of the Son of God, who loved me, and gave himself for me.

GALATIANS 2:20

The success of life does not depend upon effort, but upon the presence and power of the One Who lives His life in me and through me.

JOYCE MEYER

*A*nd in that day ye shall ask me nothing. Verily, verily, I say unto you, Whatsoever ye shall ask the Father in my name, he will give it you.

JOHN 16:23

When we go to the throne of grace in prayer, it is as though Jesus were going there, for we go in His name.

E. W. KENYON

But you are God's "chosen generation," his "royal priesthood", his "holy nation", his "peculiar people" — all the old titles of God's people now belong to you.

1 PETER 2:9 PHILLIPS

Not only am I a new creature, a child of God, a joint-heir with Jesus Christ, the righteousness of God, a king who rules and reigns in life, but I am also a priest.

BUDDY HARRISON

And whatsoever ye shall ask in my name, that will I do, that the Father may be glorified in the Son.

JOHN 14:13

When we pray, we come before the Father's throne in Jesus' name. We cannot obtain an audience with the Father except as we come to Him in the name of His Son.

KATHRYN KUHLMAN

*F*or with the heart man believeth unto righteousness; and with the mouth confession is made unto salvation.

ROMANS 10:10

Through salvation God has restored man to a place of fellowship and communion and given back to him blessings and benefits that were lost when Adam transgressed against God.

LESTER SUMRALL

What we have seen and heard we proclaim to you also, that you also may have fellowship with us; and indeed our fellowship is with the Father, and with His Son Jesus Christ.
1 JOHN 1:3 NAS

We all know that we become like those with whom we associate, so let's take advantage of associating with Father God and His Son, Jesus Christ.
MARILYN HICKEY

Let us therefore come boldly unto the throne of grace, that we may obtain mercy, and find grace to help in time of need.

HEBREWS 4:16

I can come boldly to the throne of God, without hesitation, without reservation, without any reluctance whatsoever. He is my Father, I am His child; I belong there!

BUDDY HARRISON

Moreover whom he did predestinate, them he also called: and whom he called, them he also justified: and whom he justified, them he also glorified.

What shall we then say to these things? If God be for us, who can be against us? ROMANS 8:30, 31

There is no limit to your prayer life. You have within you now all the elements that are necessary to make you all that the Father dreamed that you would be in Christ.

E. W. KENYON

*E*veryone who believes that Jesus is the Christ, out from God has been born and as a result is His child.

1 JOHN 5:1 WUEST

What is the outcome of being born of God? God's life, truth, walk, communion, fellowship, oneness, and like-mindedness becomes ours.

SMITH WIGGLESWORTH

And have put on the new man, which is renewed in knowledge after the image of him that created him.

COLOSSIANS 3:10

Jesus is the center of all. Only He is the "I am who I am." That's what living and being "In Christ" involves.

BENNY HINN

11
Dominion in Christ

If ye shall ask any thing in my name, I will do it.

JOHN 14:14

And this is the confidence that we have in him, that, if we ask any thing according to his will, he heareth us.

1 JOHN 5:14

In Christ, I can take dominion over the circumstances in my life.

*W*ho hath delivered us from the power of darkness, and hath translated us into the kingdom of his dear Son.

COLOSSIANS 1:13

Satan's dominion ended and Jesus' dominion began in our lives the moment we accepted Jesus as Lord and were born again.

KENNETH E. HAGIN

*A*nd has made us to be a kingdom and priests to serve his God and Father — to him be glory and power for ever and ever! Amen.

REVELATION 1:6 NIV

God created man to be a king. The very moment you receive Jesus Christ as your Saviour, you are made a king and a priest.

JOHN OSTEEN

*N*ow we are no longer slaves, but God's own sons. And since we are his sons, everything he has belongs to us, for that is the way God planned.

GALATIANS 4:7 TLB

If you will get to know the Lord, you will understand what all He has done for you in Jesus Christ . . . you will start to act like a child of the King . . . you will begin to learn to exercise the authority that is yours as an heir of God.

NORVEL HAYES

And these signs shall follow them that believe; In my name shall they cast out devils; they shall speak with new tongues.

MARK 16:17

The lordship of Jesus is not only over me, but it is also in me and through me.

E. W. KENYON

*F*or if because of one man's trespass (lapse, offense) death reigned through that one, much more surely will those who receive [God's] overflowing grace (unmerited favor) and the free gift of righteousness [putting them into right standing with Himself] reign as kings in life through the one Man Jesus Christ (the Messiah, the Anointed One).

ROMANS 5:17 AMP

We are to live independent of circumstances; in Christ you reign as a king in all situations.   JOHN OSTEEN

*F*or if by one man's offence death reigned by one; much more they which receive abundance of grace and of the gift of righteousness shall reign in life by one, Jesus Christ.

ROMANS 5:17

God's plan for us is that we rule and reign in life as kings: to rule and reign over circumstances, poverty, disease, and everything else that would hinder us. We reign by Jesus Christ.

KENNETH E. HAGIN

12
Authority in Christ

And Jesus came and spake unto them, saying, All power is given unto me in heaven and in earth.

MATTHEW 28:18

Behold, I give unto you power to tread on serpents and scorpions, and over all the power of the enemy: and nothing shall by any means hurt you.

LUKE 10:19

In Christ, I can walk in the same authority that He had.

Verily, verily, I say unto you, He that believeth on me, the works that I do shall he do also; and greater works than these shall he do; because I go unto my Father.

JOHN 14:12

Jesus has given us all His authority, the power of attorney to use His name, which is above every name, and told us to go do the works He did.

BUDDY HARRISON

*B*ehold! I have given you authority and power to trample upon serpents and scorpions, and [physical and mental strength and ability] over all the power that the enemy [possesses]; and nothing shall in any way harm you.

LUKE 10:19 AMP

Legally Satan was defeated at Calvary, so legally we are victors through Christ Who gave us power of attorney in Luke 10:19.

BILLYE BRIM

The thief cometh not, but for to steal, and to kill, and to destroy: I am come that they might have life, and that they might have it more abundantly.

JOHN 10:10

Jesus has come that we may have life. He has come to destroy and take away those things Satan perpetrated upon man. He came to restore man to his rightful authority.

CHARLES CAPPS

And now you see that I have given you the power to tread underfoot snakes and scorpions and all the forces of the enemy, and nothing will ever harm you.

LUKE 10:19 NEB

Just as God anointed Jesus with the Holy Spirit and gave Him power and authority to destroy the works of the devil, He has given us power and authority over all the power of the enemy.

ROD PARSLEY

*A*nd what is the exceeding greatness of his power to us-ward who believe, according to the working of his mighty power.

EPHESIANS 1:19

Unless we know who we are and what we can do by the power of Jesus Christ, Satan will have continuous victories in our lives.

JOHN OSTEEN

Let us therefore come boldly unto the throne of grace, that we may obtain mercy, and find grace to help in time of need.

HEBREWS 4:16

The glorified Christ delegated authority to men in this earth . . . we can tap the heavens. We can go before the throne of God.

CHARLES CAPPS

In whom also we have obtained an inheritance, being predestinated according to the purpose of him who worketh all things after the counsel of his own will.

EPHESIANS 1:11

Once you know who you are in Christ, once you realize your authority as a believer and the significance of your inheritance as a saint, there is a real cause for rejoicing.

JERRY SAVELLE

Now then we are ambassadors for Christ, as though God did beseech you by us: we pray you in Christ's stead, be ye reconciled to God.

2 CORINTHIANS 5:20

As a new creation in Christ, you have the name of Jesus, the Word of God, and the Spirit of God to enable you to stand and minister in the place of Jesus.

KENNETH COPELAND

Forasmuch then as the children are partakers of flesh and blood, he also himself likewise took part of the same; that through death he might destroy him that had the power of death, that is, the devil.

HEBREWS 2:14

Jesus conquered Satan through the work of the cross and resurrection and then gave us the rightful authority to use His name and see the devil run from us.

BOB YANDIAN

*A*nd Jesus came and spake unto them, saying, All power is given unto me in heaven and in earth.

MATTHEW 28:18

When we realize that the authority that belongs to Christ also belongs to individual members of the Body of Christ and is available to us, our lives will be revolutionized.

KENNETH E. HAGIN

13
Power in Christ

And they overcame him by the blood of the Lamb, and by the word of their testimony; and they loved not their lives unto the death.

REVELATION 12:11

In Christ, I have the power to be an overcomer in this life.

We have all benefited from the rich blessings he brought to us — blessing upon blessing heaped upon us!

JOHN 1:16 TLB

All the glory and power that Jesus knows at the throne of God, all the wonders of His overcoming grace, all the marvel of the greatness of His power, is yours to receive through faith.

JOHN G. LAKE

Therefore God raised him high and conferred on him a Name above all names.

PHILIPPIANS 2:9 MOFFATT

The Lord is the ever-present I Am. Everything we need, or ever will need. His name is Jesus, and that name holds power . . . when we speak that name — Jesus! — power is instantly made available to us.

JOYCE MEYER

Who being the brightness of his glory, and the express image of his person, and upholding all things by the word of his power, when he had by himself purged our sins, sat down on the right hand of the Majesty on high. HEBREWS 1:3

When we speak the Word of God, in the authority given to us, power is released! BUDDY HARRISON

I have given you authority to trample on snakes and scorpions and to overcome all the power of the enemy; nothing will harm you.

LUKE 10:19 NIV

God has given you His power and authority — His Word, His name, and His Spirit.

BILLY JOE DAUGHERTY

*A*nd hath raised us up together, and made us sit together in heavenly places in Christ Jesus.

EPHESIANS 2:6

When He ascended to heaven, He gave you power to overcome on earth.

ROD PARSLEY

I am crucified with Christ: nevertheless I live; yet not I, but Christ liveth in me: and the life which I now live in the flesh I live by the faith of the Son of God, who loved me, and gave himself for me.

GALATIANS 2:20

Jesus Christ dwells in us. We are God's power-house.

MARIA WOODWORTH-ETTER

Now it is God who makes both us and you stand firm in Christ. He anointed us.

2 CORINTHIANS 1:21 NIV

Instead of always stumbling or falling, you can be walking just like Jesus walked: in the power and anointing of Almighty God.

KEITH BUTLER

Wherefore God also hath highly exalted him, and given him a name which is above every name.

PHILIPPIANS 2:9

When we do the works of Jesus and use His name, we walk in great dynamic power — dynamite kind of power.

BUDDY HARRISON

In Him we also were made [God's] heritage (portion) and we obtained an inheritance; for we had been foreordained (chosen and appointed beforehand) in accordance with His purpose, Who works out everything in agreement with the counsel and design of His [own] will.

EPHESIANS 1:11 AMP

You have inherited the resources of God's power and ability to back you and to establish your success in the earth.   GLORIA COPELAND

*F*or in him dwelleth all the fulness of the Godhead bodily. And ye are complete in him, which is the head of all principality and power.

COLOSSIANS 2:9, 10

With the Godhead within, you can do anything God says you can do in His Word. He will not do it for you. The choices are yours.

FREDERICK K. C. PRICE

But grow in grace (undeserved favor, spiritual strength) and recognition and knowledge and understanding of our Lord and Savior Jesus Christ (the Messiah). To him [be] glory (honor, majesty, and splendor) both now and to the day of eternity. Amen (so be it)!

2 PETER 3:18 AMP

We should all be growing in the knowledge of the Lord, and that knowledge contained in the Word gives us greater and greater power to live a sinless life in a healthy body.   MARILYN HICKEY

For His divine power has bestowed upon us all things that [are requisite and suited] to life and godliness, through the [full, personal] knowledge of Him Who called us by and to His own glory and excellence (virtue).

2 PETER 1:3 AMP

God has given you a promise in His Word for power through the knowledge of Him so that you will be able to exercise victory in every area of your life.

KEITH BUTLER

I am strong enough for all things in Him Who strengtheneth me.

PHILIPPIANS 4:13 WORRELL

Fear goes out of the door when a person realizes he can do all things through Christ. There is just no room for torment to enter when this revelation comes.

BILLY JOE DAUGHERTY

*F*or in him we live, and move, and have our being; as certain also of your own poets have said, For we are also his offspring.

ACTS 17:28

What a vast storehouse of power! In Christ my Saviour and Lord I have life! Energy! Strength for the impossible tasks!

KENNETH E. HAGIN

14
Victory in Christ

Now thanks be unto God, which always causeth us to triumph in Christ, and maketh manifest the savour of his knowledge by us in every place.

2 CORINTHIANS 2:14

In Christ, I have the victory!

*B*ut one in a certain place testified, saying, What is man, that thou art mindful of him? or the son of man, that thou visitest him? Thou madest him a little lower than the angels; thou crownedst him with glory and honour, and didst set him over the works of thy hands.

HEBREWS 2:6, 7

Jesus died to lift you up and set you with Him in heavenly places. No matter how lowly you were before, you now have on your head a crown of glory and honor.

JOYCE MEYER

Now if we are children, then we are heirs — heirs of God and co-heirs with Christ, if indeed we share in his sufferings in order that we may also share in his glory.

ROMANS 8:17 NIV

We're joint-heirs with Jesus, so that means we are of the tribe of Judah also. We are praisers, and a praiser can't be defeated.

JERRY SAVELLE

Wherever I go, thank God, he makes my life a constant pageant of triumph in Christ, diffusing the perfume of his knowledge everywhere by me.

2 CORINTHIANS 2:14 MOFFATT

God has promised that He will always cause you to triumph in Christ. You are guaranteed victory over any adversity you face today.

GLORIA COPELAND

Nay, in all these things we are more than conquerors through him that loved us.

ROMANS 8:37

Major on the fact that Jesus has overcome the world. He's won! And we've been made more than conquerors through His victory!

JESSE DUPLANTIS

*A*nd in union with Christ Jesus he raised us up and enthroned us with him in the heavenly realms.

EPHESIANS 2:6 NEB

Through your exalted position in Christ, you are looking down! You are far above all principalities and powers.

JOHN OSTEEN

No, in all these things we are more than conquerors through him who loved us.

ROMANS 8:37 NIV

We're more than conquerors, not through our own efforts, but through Him. Through the Lord Jesus Christ.

KATHRYN KUHLMAN

*W*hom resist stedfast in the faith, knowing that the same afflictions are accomplished in your brethren that are in the world.

1 Peter 5:9

When He put His heel on Satan's neck, He did it for you, and you were in Christ. Satan can holler and bellow as much as he wants to, but you withstand him in the faith of Jesus.

JOHN G. LAKE

*A*nd *having disarmed the powers and authorities, he made a public spectacle of them, triumphing over them by the cross.*

COLOSSIANS 2:15 NIV

That resurrection of Jesus is proof of our victory over the adversary. Every person who takes Christ as Saviour, in the mind of God is a victor over the adversary.

E. W. KENYON

Ye are of God, little children, and have overcome them: because greater is he that is in you, than he that is in the world.

1 JOHN 4:4

Jesus is far above all powers, and so are you, if you are in Christ, through the mighty name of Jesus, because greater is He that is in you, than He that is in the world.

CHARLES CAPPS

What, then, shall we say in response to this? If God is for us, who can be against us?

ROMANS 8:31 NIV

Quit looking at what the devil has done and start looking at what God has done! He's made you more than a conqueror! If He's for you, who can be against you?

JESSE DUPLANTIS

145

Rooted and built up in him, and stablished in the faith, as ye have been taught, abounding therein with thanksgiving.

COLOSSIANS 2:7

I am established by faith on the basis of the Word of God. That is what roots me in Christ. When the winds of adversity blow, I remain steady.

FREDERICK K. C. PRICE

But thanks be to God! He gives us the victory through our Lord Jesus Christ.

1 CORINTHIANS 15:57 NIV

Your Father wants you to be victorious in this life and enjoy all the rights and privileges that Jesus purchased for you.

GLORIA COPELAND

If then you have been raised with Christ [to a new life, thus sharing His resurrection from the dead], aim at and seek the [rich, eternal treasures] that are above, where Christ is, seated at the right hand of God. COLOSSIANS 3:1 AMP

The Word says you are risen with Christ, God sees you on top of frustration, on top of temptation, on top of persecution, on top of sickness and disease and on top of hatred and prejudice.

FREDERICK K. C. PRICE

I have strength for all things in Christ Who empowers me [I am ready for anything and equal to anything through Him Who infuses inner strength into me; I am self-sufficient in Christ's sufficiency].

PHILIPPIANS 4:13 AMP

I am not the victim, I am the victor. I can do all things through Christ Who strengthens me. The Spirit of the living God indwells my being, and greater is He Who is in me than he who is in the world.

JERRY SAVELLE

The thief cometh not, but for to steal, and to kill, and to destroy: I am come that they might have life, and that they might have it more abundantly.

JOHN 10:10

God has a realm of divine life opening up to us where there are boundless possibilities, where there is limitless power, where there are untold resources, where we have victory over all the power of the devil.

SMITH WIGGLESWORTH

Now unto him that is able to keep you from falling, and to present you faultless before the presence of his glory with exceeding joy.

JUDE 1:24

Through the knowledge of what Jesus has provided for us, and our acceptance of His work on the cross, we have been placed in the position where we will never have to stumble or fall again!

KEITH BUTLER

*N*ay, in all these things we are more than conquerors through him that loved us.

ROMANS 8:37

No matter what you have done or how you may have failed, you are more than a conqueror. God the Father has made you to be a conqueror through the Son, Jesus Christ.

BILLY JOE DAUGHERTY

In the face of all this, what is there left to say? If God is for us, who can be against us?

ROMANS 8:31 PHILLIPS

For you to truly rejoice, you must know where you stand with God . . . you must know that God is on your side . . . and if God be for you who could dare be against you?

JERRY SAVELLE

I have written unto you, fathers, because ye have known him that is from the beginning. I have written unto you, young men, because ye are strong, and the word of God abideth in you, and ye have overcome the wicked one.

1 JOHN 2:14

The only way Christians will be able to overcome the onslaught of the enemy that comes against them, as those called by Christ's name, is to operate in the Word.   FREDERICK K. C. PRICE

But thanks be to God, who gives us the victory through our Lord Jesus Christ.

1 Corinthians 15:57 NAS

It is a fact that you have absolute victory in Jesus Christ, a gift to be received from Him. Think it, dream it, talk it, and you will live it.

Billy Joe Daugherty

Bible References

Scripture quotations marked (AMP) are taken from *The Amplified Bible. Old Testament* copyright © 1965, 1987 by The Zondervan Corporation, Grand Rapids, Michigan. New Testament copyright © 1954, 1958, 1987 by The Lockman Foundation, La Habra, California. Used by permission.

Scripture quotations marked (Moffatt) are taken from *The Bible. A New Translation*. Copyright © 1950, 1952, 1953, 1954 by James A. R. Moffatt, Harper & Row Publishers, Inc., New York, New York.

Scripture quotations marked (NIV) are taken from the *Holy Bible, New International Version*®. NIV®. Copyright © 1973, 1978, 1984 by International Bible Society. Used by permission of Zondervan Publishing House. All rights reserved.

Verses marked (TLB) are taken from *The Living Bible* copyright © 1971. Used by permission of Tyndale House Publishers, Inc., Wheaton, Illinois 60189. All rights reserved.

Scripture quotations marked (NAS) are taken from the *New American Standard Bible*®. Copyright © The

References

Bosworth, F. F. *Christ the Healer.* Old Tappan, New Jersey: Power Books, Fleming H. Revell Company, 1973.

Butler, Keith. *Success Strategies From Heaven.* Tulsa, Oklahoma: Harrison House Publishers, 1995.

Copeland, Kenneth. *The Force of Righteousness.* Fort Worth, Texas: KCP Publications, 1984.

Copeland, Kenneth. *Now Are We In Christ Jesus.* Fort Worth, Texas: KCP Publications, 1980.

Duplantis, Jesse. *The Ministry of Cheerfulness.* Tulsa, Oklahoma: Harrison House Publishers, 1993.

Hagin, Kenneth E. *The Believer's Authority.* Broken Arrow, Oklahoma: Faith Library Publications, 1984.

Hagin, Kenneth E. *In Him.* Broken Arrow, Oklahoma: Faith Library Publications, 1975.

Kenyon, E. W. *Identification.* Lynnwood, Washington: Kenyon's Gospel Publishing Society, Inc., 1968.

Kenyon, E. W. *In His Presence.* Lynnwood, Washington: Kenyon's Gospel Publishing Society, Inc., 1969.

Kenyon, E. W. *New Creation Realities*. Lynnwood, Washington: Kenyon's Gospel Publishing Society, Inc., 1945, 1964.

Lake, *John G. John G. Lake: His Life, His Sermons, His Boldness of Faith*. Fort Worth, Texas: KCP Publications, 1994.

Nelson, P. C. *Bible Doctrines*. Springfield, Missouri: Radiant Books, Gospel Publishing House, 1948, 1971, 1981.

Osteen, John. *Reigning in Life As a King*. Houston, Texas: John Osteen Publications, 1984.

Parsley, Rod. *Serious Survival Strategies*. Columbus, Ohio: Results Publishing, 1992.

Price, Fred. *The Victorious Overcoming Life*. Los Angeles, California: Crenshaw Christian Center Publishing, 1993.

Woodworth-Etter, Maria. *A Diary of Signs and Wonders*. Tulsa, Oklahoma: Harrison House Publishers, 1916.

Yandian, Bob. *Ephesians: The Maturing of the Saints*. Tulsa, Oklahoma: Harrison House Publishers, 1985.

The Harrison House Vision

Proclaiming the truth and the power
Of the Gospel of Jesus Christ
With excellence;

Challenging Christians to
Live victoriously,
Grow spiritually,
Know God intimately.